Spiritual Nurturing

How To Help Your
Child Grow Spiritually

Darlene Carpenter

Published by Carpenter Shop Resources
PO Box 292175, Lewisville, TX 75029

Unless otherwise noted, all scripture quotations
are taken from the Holy Bible, New International Version,
Copyright © 1973, 1978, 1978, 1984 by the International Bible Society.
Used by permission of Zondervan Bible Publishers.

Library of Congress Catalog Card Number: 99-90357
ISBN 0-9671274-0-8

Book design by Buell Design

Printed in the United States of America

Dedicated to

Barbara, Scott and Judy

*Nurturing you
has brought joy and fulfillment
to our lives*

Table of Contents

INTRODUCTION

*"When God wants a great work done in the world
or a great wrong righted,
He goes about it in a very unusual way.
He doesn't stir up His earthquakes
or send forth His thunderbolts.
Instead, He has a helpless baby born,
perhaps in a simple home and of some obscure parents.
And then God puts the idea into the parents' hearts,
and they put it into the baby's mind.
And then God waits.
The greatest forces in the world are not
the earthquakes and the thunderbolts.
The greatest forces in the world are babies!"*

E. T. Sullivan

Dan and I were living in Denver, Colorado and had been married about 10 months when a doctor said the heart-wrenching words, "You'll never be able to have children!" Tears blurred my vision as I sat in his office and the thought of not being a mother slowly penetrated my mind. I sobbed all the way back to our small apartment, not wanting to believe the words I'd heard.

The doctor made his statement based on his knowledge, experience and background. However, God had something else in mind. Ten months later, on February 13, 1968, our first child, Barbie, was born and our lives have never been the same. We became very aware of the awesome responsibility that was before us. As she grew and our other two children, Scott and Judy, joined our family, we knew that it was up to us to plant the ideas in their minds that would influence them to become wholesome, mature adults. We learned that we could determine objectives that would give us focus and purpose in our role as parents.

We were very conscious of the fact that the spiritual area is the most important because it impacts every other dimension of a child's life. Each child's personal relationship with God is the most important decision of his or her life. It will determine the way they live their life and make decisions as an adult and is the basis on which they will build their entire system of values, morals and ethics.

As a parent, you are the most important person molding your child's faith. You have the choice of either "letting things happen by accident" or "making things happen on purpose." The process of instilling in your child the spiritual teachings and values you treasure can be accomplished by planning.

Webster defines nurture as "to help grow or develop; train; the environmental influences on a person as distinguished from his nature or heredity." In Ephesians 6:4, Paul tells us to bring our children up "in the nurture and admonition of the Lord." (KJV) The NIV Bible says, "bring them up in the training and instruction of the Lord." Nurturing our children spiritually is not a suggestion – it's a command!

This book will give you some guidelines and ideas to assist you as you look for down-to-earth, tangible ways to nurture your child spiritually. Read the suggestions, adapt them as needed to fit your family and use them as a springboard for ideas of your own.

Part One

Focus and Direction

"You may delay,
but time will not."
— Ben Franklin

WRITING A
SPIRITUAL MISSION STATEMENT

For several weeks we had been anticipating our vacation. Barbie was four years old, Scott was two, and Judy just six months. We had heard reports about the wonderful resorts nestled around the lakes in Northern Minnesota, so we decided that's where we'd go. Some of our friends asked us the name of the resort we had chosen. We didn't know yet! Others warned us that we needed to make reservations. We didn't do it!

The day of our departure arrived and we packed everything into the station wagon. We had never been to a resort before so we weren't sure what we would need. But we tried to be as thorough in our packing as possible, especially making sure we had included the bamboo fishing poles.

As we began our trip out of Minneapolis, the whole northern half of the state stretched ahead as a possible destination. Detroit Lakes, Brainerd, Bemidji, Grand Rapids . . . which one should it be? We chose Brainerd! As we got closer, we began looking for signs advertising resorts in the area.

The first place we stopped looked great tucked neatly under the trees only steps from the beach. Unfortunately, they didn't have any vacancies. The second stop was a "Cadillac resort" complete with golf courses and a helicopter pad for the rich and famous, which was far beyond our "Model T budget." The third sign pointed in a direction that seemed to be away from the lake but we decided to investigate it anyway. We were right. It had nice cabins but the lakefront was a distance away.

As we continued our search, we started to wonder if

we'd find just the right spot. The question that plagued our minds was, "Would we know the right one when we did see it?" We never had really discussed exactly what we were looking for in our first resort vacation.

After what seemed like several hours of wandering along country roads and stopping at numerous places, we chose Sunset View Resort on Long Lake. It was right on the lake, fit our budget, had a nice dock from which to fish, and had a genuine family atmosphere. Everything turned out fine and we had a great time.

In retrospect, we've wondered what would have happened if we had taken the advice of our friends and determined our destination before we left. Would we have found an even better vacation spot if we had made reservations? Dan had intended to call places for information before we left, but just never quite got around to it. While we enjoy spontaneity and flexibility, we admit that planning ahead would have been much better than the mounting anxiety we experienced as we wandered from resort to resort.

Parents often approach the spiritual nurturing of their children in much the same way we approached our vacation. For nine months they anticipate the birth of their child with great excitement. Their desire is for this child to grow up to be a responsible person with strong moral, ethical and spiritual values.

However, they have not taken the time to actually determine what that means. When the baby arrives, the years before he will leave home stretch endlessly before them. There seems to be plenty of time to think about what they want to teach him spiritually. Sadly, those years slip by all too quickly. Suddenly he is ready to leave for college, a job or marriage. They realize they haven't taught him all they had intended; he isn't strong spiritually and they may fear for his future.

One of the traditions our family has enjoyed for many

years is putting together a 1000-piece puzzle over the Christmas holidays. We follow the same procedure every year – buying a new puzzle, setting up the folding table and dumping out all the pieces. We find the old worn-out cookie sheets and divide the pieces into those pans according to the major colors. While everyone enjoys this Christmas ritual, Judy and I take it the most seriously. Usually at some point during the holidays we will stay up until the wee hours of the morning to finish it. We've learned that the pleasure of successfully completing our puzzle lies in one small object – the picture on the cover of the box! We refer to it constantly as we put the hundreds of random pieces in the right place to duplicate that picture. Setting the cover conspicuously at the edge of the table keeps us on track to accomplish our goal.

The same is true of helping children grow spiritually. A Spiritual Mission Statement (I like to call it a SMS) will define the end result you're trying to attain. When you know what the completed picture looks like – what you want to instill in your child before she is 18 or leaves home – it'll be much easier to plan and choose the right things to help you reach that result. Whatever the age of your child, now is the time to formulate a SMS.

Physical growth of a child is one part of his development. To achieve that growth there are several areas to consider, including balanced nutrition, adequate sleep, exercise, medical and dental care, etc. While one parent may feel that nutrition is the most important area and spend a great deal of time planning and preparing the best meals, another parent may feel that exercise should take a higher priority. Both are important for optimum health, but each parent will approach the balance with a different perspective and emphasis.

The same is true of spiritual growth. It is one part of a child's development, but there are many areas to consider which can contribute to that growth. In order to write a SMS, the first step is to determine exactly what you personally believe to be most important to the spiritual growth of your child. Some suggested areas to help you get started are . . .

- memorizing scripture
- experiencing a personal walk with God through prayer
- demonstrating high moral and ethical principles
- loving God's Word – both academically and in personal application
- having a deep love for the church
- developing and exemplifying character qualities such as kindness, faith, submission to God, trust, patience, peace, tolerance, purity, love for others, gentleness, gratitude, self-control, joy, forgiveness, humility and truthfulness
- understanding and living according to God's will
- showing a concern for the spiritual needs of others
- developing a concern for missions and missionaries
- displaying a sensitivity toward spiritual things
- desiring to put God first in all of life's decisions

This is by no means a complete list, but its purpose is to act as a catalyst for you to think of the things that are important to you. Having a balance in teaching your children spiritual values is important, but you will find that certain areas will become a higher priority to you. Before you begin, ask yourself these questions:

"If my child were a young adult ready to leave home today . . .

    . . . what would I want her to have experienced spiritually?

    . . . what are the most important spiritual characteristics she would display?

    . . . what would cause me to be able to release her with confidence that she was prepared spiritually to meet the challenges of life?"

Now begin to write a SMS following these 3 steps:

Step 1: Write ten things you feel are important to the spiritual growth of your child on the lines below, using the ideas already listed along with your own.

1._____

2._____

3._____

4._____

5._____

6._____

7._____

8._____

9._____

10._____

Step 2. By completing the list above you've already thought through and defined your spiritual value system. Being conscious of your personal priorities will help you provide opportunities in your child's life for development in these areas. Now choose the three items that are your very top priority. The SMS should reflect the areas that you feel are non-negotiable – the three highest-priority items. Write these three choices below.

1._____

2._____

3._____

Step 3: Use the three items you've just listed and write them into a one-sentence SMS. Include your child's name in the statement and make it very personal. If you have more than one child, write a separate statement for each of them. Whether you write a completely different statement for each child or use the same one for all of your children, DO write it out individually for each child. There is something meaningful in having it before you with the individual child's name in his or her statement.

Below are some sample *Spiritual Mission Statements*. These should give you a starting point to write your own.

Our / my SMS for . . .

> . . . Becky is for her to have a personal relationship with Christ, love the scriptures and have a concern for the needs of others.

> . . . Jill is for her to exemplify the fruit of the Spirit in her life and have a love for the church.

> . . . John is for him to know Christ as his personal Savior and develop a concern for missions and outreach to others.

> . . . Sarah is for her to have a personal relationship with Christ, a teachable attitude and a concern for the spiritual needs of others.

> . . . Tim is for him to experience God's forgiveness, learn to live a life of deep faith and treat others with love and kindness.

> . . . Anne is for her to learn to love the scriptures, memorize its words consistently and have prayer as a guiding principle of her life.

. . . David is for him to progress toward spiritual maturity through his knowledge of scripture and prayer and for the decisions he makes to be according to God's will for his life.

. . . Randy is for him to love God's Word and apply its principles to his life, live a life of purity and practice self-control in his relationships.

. . . Josh is for him to grow to be spiritually mature with a deep desire to be in the center of God's will for his life.

. . . Carrie is for her to be sensitive to the commands of scripture, consistently experience answers to her prayer and grow in her tolerance toward others.

Review your list of three top priority items that you listed in step two on page 15. Incorporate these items into one sentence and write them as your child's SMS below.

_____

_____

_____

_____

_____

_____

_____

Signature

_____

Date

When you have completed your SMS, print it on an index card and keep it in a place where you'll see it every day, such as in your Bible, on your mirror or on a bulletin board close to the kitchen table. Read it, memorize it and make it a part of your daily life!

Part Two

Ideas, Thoughts and
Brainstorms

"You always get out what you put in.
Plant apple seeds and you get apple trees;
plant the seeds of great ideas,
and you will get great individuals"

— Denis Waitley

Some time ago, I attended a bridal shower where a good friend, Jeanette, gave a short devotional to the guests. She told stories of her own experiences as a new wife whose husband was busy going to graduate school. In recounting some of her own struggles, one comment she made was, "Remember, you are not your husband's holy spirit!" She reminded us that God does His work through the Holy Spirit in our spouse's life and it is not up to us to determine what He should be doing. The same is true in our children's lives. God will work in your child's life through the Holy Spirit, but as parents, it is our responsibility to provide the atmosphere and environment where He can do His work in their tender hearts.

The greatest privilege of any parent is to lead their child to Christ; to explain the way of salvation and pray with them to accept Jesus. The Holy Spirit is the One who convicts of sin and the child needs to make that decision to follow Christ on his own. But by being sensitive to God's work in your child's life there is no greater joy than to be the one to share that experience with them. Just as in every other part of a child's life, there is not a particular age or time when this may happen – everyone has their own unique experience.

Barbie told me that she had accepted Jesus in Sunday School and when we would talk about it, she assured me that she was a Christian. However, one New Year's Eve when she was a teenager, the house was quiet and everyone was in bed when I heard her call me to her bedroom. My first reaction was that she was sick, so I rushed to her room. When I sat down on her bed, she said, "Oh, Mom, I'm so scared! I'm not sure I'm a Christian!" My heart reached out to her as I thought of my own experience. I accepted Christ when I was only five years old, but as a teenager I too had faced doubts and lacked assurance. We sat on her bed and talked for a long time. After reading some verses and praying together, her face lit up. Her burden had been lifted! The first thing we did was to wake her Dad and tell him the good news.

Our family went through the same thing that most other families face – how to keep those kids snugly in bed at night after being tucked in. Sometimes we were successful; other times there would be extended bathroom or drink "emergencies." Scott was eight years old and had been tucked in for the night. I was sitting on the sofa reading a magazine when he came slowly into the room, sat down close to me and snuggled up tight. I asked him what he needed and tears immediately filled his eyes. As he started to cry, he said, "Mommy, I want to be a Christian." That evening, in our living room, Scott joined the family of God!

Judy, our youngest, was my constant shadow. While the older two kids were in school she and I would go shopping and run errands. We would chatter together as we drove along or as we debated about buying the red or pink fabric, the lettuce or the cabbage. Judy was a child who could ask ten questions before we could even begin to answer the first five. On this particular day I'd taken her along to do some preliminary suit shopping for Dan. There had been a newspaper ad for a suit sale at a store at the other end of Minneapolis so we had plenty of time to talk as we drove along. Accepting Jesus was on her mind and we talked about it during our entire trip. In fact, for several days she had been asking questions and talking about it. Since she was only five years old, I didn't want to say anything that would push her into a decision. On the other hand, I knew her little heart was tender and that the Holy Spirit was speaking to her. As we parked in front of the store, I assured her that she could accept Jesus any time she was ready. She looked me square in the eye and said, "Well, I think I should do it right now!" So in front of a store, in a strange part of the city, we sat in our car and Judy prayed to become part of God's family!

I will always treasure those moments with my children.

Those experiences are highlights of my parenting career!

I would challenge every parent to prepare the ground-work and provide the atmosphere in your home so the Holy Spirit can easily do His work. Many people make their decision to follow Christ in places other than at home. But the chances are pretty strong that at some point in time, the Holy Spirit has been speaking to their hearts while they are at home. While you may or may not have the opportunity to actually lead your child to Christ, your home is the place where the groundwork can be laid and where unlimited nurturing can take place.

After you have written the SMS for your child, the second step is to find things to do to help you reach that objective. This book will give hundreds of ideas to help you get started. They are divided into 12 areas with suggestions for different ages of children. If an idea, product or service is specifically for a particular age you will find that noted as well. The areas are: scripture, prayer, church, family devotions, books and magazines, cassette tapes, video tapes, missions and outreach, music, special events, activities, and example and influence.

Select and implement those things that you feel would help you reach the SMS you've written and use the rest as a springboard for ideas of your own — things you think of that fit your family, your time restraints, the age of your child and your church background. These suggestions include things we did in our own family, some that we wish we had done, and others that I simply feel are worthwhile.

Where specific titles of products or services are suggested, you will find in parentheses the name of the publisher or company that produces and/or distributes it. In the back of the book is a list of these providers with their addresses. Christian bookstores will usually have the product suggested or will order it for you. Many items can also be ordered over the Internet through a publisher, distributor or bookstore.

Helping Your Child Grow Spiritually Through
SCRIPTURE

Of all the ways to help your child grow spiritually, scripture and prayer should be at the top of the list. People whose lives are built on scriptural principles are the most productive, happy and satisfied. Laying a solid foundation of truths from scripture needs to begin at a very early age. Make the Bible the center of your family life. The biblical principles you teach your child will be a very important factor in the decisions he makes both now and later in life.

- The single most important thing we did to incorporate scripture into our family's life was to memorize a verse a week around the table at mealtime. At the beginning of the year, Dan and I would decide which verses to learn. We'd begin by selecting 12 different topics – one for each month. Then we'd simply choose four or five verses to memorize about that subject. When the children were young we concentrated on very short verses. As they got older, the verses got longer. As with other busy young families, we didn't sit down to three meals a day together, but we'd always say the verse in the evening when we had dinner together and as often as possible at breakfast and lunch. As we would think about it during the week – riding in the car, taking a walk, etc. - we'd try to make a game of it and ask, "What's our verse for this week?" It's amazing how quickly verses can be memorized and retained through this kind of <u>spaced repetition</u>. I'm the first to admit, however, that the kids almost always knew the verse well by the end of the week, but I'd still be struggling more times than I'd like to admit.

  The first time I saw the tangible display of the

benefits of this kind of memorizing came when Barbie was about seven years old. We were talking to her Sunday School teacher after church and with her arm around Barbie, she said, "What have you done to this child?" Of course we wondered what she meant. She went on to explain that for the last four Sundays Barbie already knew the verses they were studying.

Our kids attended a Christian school and in seventh grade there was an emphasis on scripture memory in their Bible class. Even though Scott was a good student, I noticed he wasn't working on his memory verses. When I mentioned it to him, he just said, "Oh, I already know most of them." We had learned them around the table so he just had to review them!

• Set aside an hour or two to select the verses your family is going to memorize for the next month, six months or year. If you feel that a verse a week is too much, start out with a verse a month instead. Write down the references where they'll be handy each time you're ready to begin a new one. (In the "Getting Started" section of this book, a simple, specific plan will be given to show how easy it is to have the verses at your fingertips each week.) To help in your selection, use the subject index or concordance in the back of your Bible. If it doesn't have one, or if you would like a more comprehensive listing, purchase a book such as:

　The New Strong's Exhaustive Concordance of the Bible
　　(Thomas Nelson)
　Three-In-One Bible Reference Companion
　　(Thomas Nelson)
　NAVES Topical Bible (Zondervan)
　The New Strong's Concise Concordance of the Bible
　　(Thomas Nelson)
　Thomas Nelson's Quick Reference Bible Concordance
　　(Thomas Nelson)

- On the following pages are some suggested subjects and verses you could start memorizing together using the spaced repetition concept. If your child is very young a program of scripture memory can still be started. Simply use short portions of a verse instead of something longer. The italicized parts of the verses below are ideas of how to use just a meaningful phrase for little ones.

Children

Mark 10:14   *Let the little children come to me,* and do not hinder them, for the kingdom of God belongs to such as these.

Ephesians 6:1   *Children, obey your parents* in the Lord, for this is right.

Exodus 20:12   *Honor your father and your mother,* so that you may live long in the land the Lord your God is giving you.

Eccles. 12:1   *Remember your creator in the days of your youth,* before the days of trouble come and the years approach when you say, "I find no pleasure in them."

Salvation

John 3:16   *For God so loved the world that he gave his one and only Son,* that whoever believes in him shall not perish but have eternal life.

Romans 3:23   *For all have sinned* and fall short of the glory of God.

Romans 6:23   For the wages of sin is death, but *the gift of God is eternal life* in Christ Jesus our Lord.

Romans 10:13   *Everyone who calls on the name of the Lord will be saved.*

John 1:12   *Yet to all who received him,* to those who believed in his name, *he gave the right to become children of God.*

Word of God

Matthew 24:35	Heaven and earth will pass away, but *my words will never pass away.*
James 1:22	*Do not merely listen to the word,* and so deceive yourselves. Do what it says.
Psalms 119:105	*Your word is a lamp to my feet* and a light for my path.
Psalms 119:11	*I have hidden your word in my heart* that I might not sin against you.

Prayer

Jeremiah 33:3	*Call to me and I will answer you* and tell you great and unsearchable things you do not know.
Matthew 7:7	*Ask and it will be given to you;* seek and you will find; knock and the door will be opened to you.
I John 5:14	This is the confidence we have in approaching God: that *if we ask anything according to his will, he hears us.*
Matthew 21:22	*If you believe, you will receive whatever you ask for in prayer.*

Love

Matthew 22:37	*Love the Lord your God* with all your heart and with all your soul and with all your mind.
I Corinth. 13:4	Love is patient, *love is kind.* It does not envy, it does not boast, it is not proud.
I John 4:7	Dear friends, *let us love one another,* for love comes from God. Everyone who loves has been born of God and knows God.
I John 4:8	Whoever does not love does not know God, because *God is love.*
Psalms 18:1	*I love you, O Lord,* my strength.

Praise

Psalms 92:1   *It is good to praise the Lord* and to make music to your name, O Most High.

Psalms 34:1   I will extol the Lord at all times; *his praise will always be on my lips.*

Psalms 145:3   *Great is the Lord and most worthy of praise;* his greatness no one can fathom.

Psalms 100:1-2   *Shout for joy to the Lord,* all the earth. Worship the Lord with gladness; come before him with joyful songs.

Trust

Psalms 28:7   *The Lord is my strength* and my shield; my heart trusts in him, and I am helped.

Psalms 56:3   When I am afraid, *I will trust in you.*

Proverbs 3:5   *Trust in the Lord with all your heart* and lean not on your own understanding.

Proverbs 29:25   Fear of man will prove to be a snare, but *whoever trusts in the Lord is kept safe.*

Isaiah 26:4   *Trust in the Lord forever,* for the Lord, the Lord, is the Rock eternal.

Faith

Romans 10:17   Consequently, *faith comes from hearing the message,* and the message is heard through the word of Christ.

Hebrews 11:1   *Now faith is being sure of what we hope for* and certain of what we do not see.

Hebrews 11:6   And *without faith it is impossible to please God,* because anyone who comes to him must believe that he exists and that he rewards those who earnestly seek him.

Romans 5:1   Therefore, since we have been justified through faith, *we have peace with God* through our Lord Jesus Christ.

Comfort

Psalms 46:1   *God is our refuge and strength*, an ever-present help in trouble.

Matthew 11:28   Come to me, all you who are weary and burdened, and *I will give you rest.*

John 14:1   Do not let your hearts be troubled. *Trust in God; trust also in me.*

I Peter 5:7   Cast all your anxiety on him because *he cares for you.*

Forgiveness

I John 1:9   If we confess our sins, *he is faithful and just and will forgive us our sins* and purify us from all unrighteousness.

Psalms 103:2-3   *Praise the Lord,* O my soul, and forget not all his benefits – *who forgives all your sins* and heals all your diseases.

Ephesians 4:32   *Be kind* and compassionate *to one another,* forgiving each other, just as in Christ God forgave you.

Psalms 86:5   *You are forgiving and good, O Lord,* abounding in love to all who call to you.

Holy Spirit

I John 4:13   We know that we live in him and he in us, because *he has given us of his Spirit.*

I John 3:24   *Those who obey his commands live in him,* and he in them. And this is how we know that he lives in us: We know it by the Spirit he gave us.

Romans 8:14   Because *those who are led by the Spirit of God are sons of God.*

Galat. 5:22–23   *But the fruit of the Spirit is love,* joy, peace, patience, kindness, goodness, faithfulness, gentleness and self-control. Against such things there is no law.

Christmas

Matthew 1:21	She will give birth to a son, and *you are to give him the name Jesus,* because he will save his people from their sins.
Luke 2:10	But the angel said to them, *"Do not be afraid. I bring you good news of great joy that will be for all the people."*
Luke 2:11	Today in the town of David a Savior has been born to you; *he is Christ the Lord.*
Luke 2:52	And *Jesus grew* in wisdom and stature, and *in favor with God and men.*

• You could also memorize an entire chapter such as I Corinthians 13. Divide it into verses or manageable segments and plan how much to memorize each week.

• Give each verse a title and write it out on an index card. Read it alternately between family members during your devotional time, discuss the verse and review a little every day. You could also use verses already titled and printed such as those in *The Wheel* (NavPress). A very valuable resource!

• Collect pictures and photos of Bible places and people – both historical and contemporary. Make a special notebook of them, mount them on construction paper or cardboard, make a collage, or post them on the refrigerator or in your child's room.

• Memorize and review the books of the Bible together. You might want to put the names on flash cards or use the *Keyword Learning Systems* (Walk Thru the Bible) to help remember them. Make a game of it. Review them together as you take a walk, do dishes, make beds or relax on the patio.

- Play a game of memorized Bible verses. Start with A – "All things work together for good . . ." Then the next person must recite a verse beginning with B – "Be kind one to another . . ." Then on to C – "Cast all your care on Him . . ." and continue to Z.

- Have a contest to see how far your family can go in naming the books of the Old or New Testament. Go around the circle with each person naming the next book in succession.

- Make memorizing scripture fun and challenging. For instance, challenge your child to see which of you can memorize selected verses or an entire chapter first. Then plan to do something you both enjoy to celebrate when you've completed them.

- During the summer vacation, have a contest to see who can memorize the most verses. Chart each family member's progress in a creative manner. For instance, draw a thermometer for each person on a piece of tagboard. As each verse is memorized, color in another degree higher on the temperature. Or buy a small poster for each family member and make each one into a puzzle, cutting them into the same number of pieces. Put your puzzles together by mounting each of them on a piece of tagboard, pasting each piece into its appropriate place. See who can reconstruct their poster first with each piece representing one verse memorized.

- Begin reading the Bible to your infant while holding, feeding or rocking him. Long before he is able to understand the meaning, his mind is beginning to associate the importance of God and the name of Jesus as he hears those words.

- Memorize scripture using one of the following helpful tools:

    Scripture Rock – A Rock Solid Way To Learn God's Word CD or audio tape (Brentwood-Benson)

    Heart Hiders Vol. 1 – 66 full color verses on 7 topics (Off the Curb)

    Heart Hiders Flash Cards – 34 verses (Off the Curb)

    Heart Hiders Reproducible Coloring Book – 58 verses which are creatively visualized to learn while coloring (Off the Curb)

- Help your child learn to read the Bible using the *Read With Me Bible* CD-ROM (Zondervan)

- Explain the meaning of biblical terms and wording. Have a good Bible dictionary available to refer to when needed, such as:

    Holman Bible Dictionary (Broadman & Holman)

    Pictorial Bible Dictionary (Zondervan)

    The Illustrated Dictionary of the Bible (Thomas Nelson)

- Help your child understand the Bible with CD-ROMs such as:

    Scripture Sleuth – New Testament and Old Testament Trivia (Ideal / Instructional Fair)

    The Baker Bible Encyclopedia – Ages 8-12 (Baker)

    Bibleland.com – Ages 8-12 (Baker)

    New Kids Point and Play Bible – Ages 8-12 (Baker)

    The Amazing Expedition Bible – Ages 8-12 (Baker)

    Illustrated Manners and Customs of the Bible (Thomas Nelson)

    Baker Bible Dictionary for Kids (Baker)

    Baker Book of Bible People for Kids – Ages 8+ (Baker)

    The Baker Bible Handbook for Kids – Ages 8-12 (Baker)

    The Children's Bible Encyclopedia – Ages 8+ (Baker)

- When traveling, play a game of memorized verses based on billboards. The first person who sees an "A" on a billboard and can successfully recite a verse that begins with "A" gets to look for a "B". The first person to complete the alphabet (or the person who can get the farthest by a given time) wins the game.

- Make sure your child has her own Bible at an early age. Toddlers like to have a small New Testament but by the time a child is learning to read, she needs to have her own complete Bible. Some suggested ones are:
  Psalty's Kids Bible – NIV (Zondervan)
  Precious Moments Bible – NKJV (Tyndale)
  New Explorers Study Bible – NKJV (Thomas Nelson)
  The New Adventure Bible – KJV and NIV (Zondervan)
  NIrV Children's Bible – *The Beginners Bible* – Ages 6-10 (Zondervan)
  NIrV Kids' Quest Study Bible – Ages 6-10 (Zondervan)
  Life Application Bible – New Living Translation – Ages 8-12 (Tyndale)
  The One Year Bible for Kids – New Living Translation (Tyndale)
  The New Adventure Bible – NIV (Zondervan)

- Be on the alert for devotional materials that are suited to your child's age level such as:
  Spending Prime Time With God Series – Ages 10-12 (Broadman & Holman)
  Frogs in Pharoah's Bed (Tyndale)
  Caution: Dangerous Devotions (Chariot Victor)
  The Children's Daily Devotional Bible (Thomas Nelson)
  Daily Bread for Boys and Girls – Ages 6-12 (Child Evangelism)
  NIrV Kids' Devotional Bible – Ages 6-10 (Zondervan)
  Picture Bible Devotions (Chariot Victor)
  Kids' Book of Devotions – Ages 7-11 (Zondervan)

- Ask one of your church staff members for suggested devotional materials for your child's age from your denominational publisher.

- Read stories from a Bible story book onto a cassette tape for your child. She can simply listen to it or follow along by looking at the pictures in the book at the same time. If she is quite young you may want to insert a special sound indicating when the pages are to be turned. (Dan has read books to our out-of-state grandkids this way. He enjoys recording the tapes, adding special voice inflections and the girls love to receive them. They really love their Grandpa Dan stories!)

- Make a video of Bible stories. Read with great expression and look at your child through the camera. If you're reading from a book where he can follow along, talk to him at the beginning, letting him know the page number and when to turn the pages.

- Have an old-fashioned Bible drill. Make a list of verses all dealing with a particular subject for the rest of the family to race to look up and read. The person who finds the most verses first is the winner.

- Tell Bible stories to your child, or let her tell them to you using felt visuals. A wide variety of very beautiful felt stories may be purchased from *Betty Lukens* or *Little Folk Visuals*.

- Tell Bible stories to your child using puppets. You can make paper bag or finger puppets. There are also beautiful professional puppets that are available from several companies (Maher Studios, One Way Street, Puppet Factory, Son Shine Puppet Co.).

- Consider buying CD-ROMs that will help your child learn Bible stories such as:
    - *The Beginners Bible* Series – Ages 3-8 (Baker)
    - *My 100 All-Time Favorite Bible Stories* (Baker)
    - *The Birth of Jesus Activity Center* (Brighter Child)
    - *Interactive Bible for Kids* Series – Ages 3-8 (Tyndale)
    - *The Treasure Study Bible* – Ages 7+ (Kirkbride)
    - *Children's Bible – 140 Stories* – Ages 4+
        (Heaven Word)
    - *Read With Me Bible – NIV Story Bible for Children –*
        Ages 5-10 (Zondervan)
    - *Noah & the Ark and Jonah & the Whale – A Play*
        Along Storybook – Ages 3-8 (Parsons)
    - *Children's Activity Bible* – Ages 2+ (Thomas Nelson)
    - *My Play Time Friends* – Ages 3+ (Standard)
    - *God Loves Me* – Ages 3+ (Standard)
    - *God's A-Z Creatures* – Ages 3+ (Standard)
    - *Heroes of the Bible* – Ages 3+ (Standard)
    - *Time Travelers Explore the Bible* – Ages 3+ (Standard)

- Help your child understand that Jesus is the Savior who longs to have a personal, vital, living relationship with each person. Guide him into growing in that relationship daily.

Helping Your Child Grow Spiritually Through
PRAYER

As adults, we may struggle with our prayer life at times or be plagued by doubts and lack of trust. However, when children are taught to pray to a loving Heavenly Father, they have complete faith and trust in Him. As the promises of answered prayer from scripture are related to a child and his needs, they are ready to be fully accepting of them. The earlier a child is taught to pray, the easier it is for his faith to grow and mature as he experiences answers to his prayers.

- Show reverence and humility by kneeling when you pray.

- Children are great imitators and will receive their first lessons in prayer by listening to you. Let your child hear you talk to God as if He is your best friend and you have an intimate relationship. Make your prayers conversational and respectful when approaching a holy God.

- Teach the three major aspects of prayer – thanksgiving, confession and intercession.

- At an early age, help your child memorize the promises in scripture regarding prayer. The previous section in this book gave you many ideas of how to make memorization a success.

- Talk about your long range and short range prayer requests as a family. Make a list of specific prayer requests and check them off as each request is answered.

- Make a visual prayer list. Use pictures as reminders of what and who to pray for. You may want to make it into a scrapbook or maybe post it on the refrigerator or a bulletin board in your child's room or near the kitchen table.

- Teach and demonstrate that prayer can be simply a sentence at any time throughout the day. It can be verbalized out loud or can be a thought in the mind directed heavenward.

- Recall happy events of the day at bedtime and pray about them. Or, maybe there haven't been any happy events and it's been a difficult day. Pray about that as well. What better way to close out a day with your child than to thank God for the good things and to leave the concerns in His care for the night?

- Teach your child to use a prayer journal. It can be as simple as a spiral notebook that she can use to write out her prayers, make a list of her personal prayer concerns, write answers, etc. She could also use it to paste in pictures of her family and friends with notations beside each picture of special prayer requests. She should make it very personal and a visual reminder of her prayers and life with God.

- Before our kids started school, we would sometimes accompany Dan on business trips. After we got the car packed and everyone settled we would always try to pray together before we left. We wanted to impress on them that God was real not only in their usual surroundings but was with us regardless of where we were going. Make a habit of praying together before leaving for special outings, trips or activities.

- When you're out of town on business, talk with your child every day on the phone. Find out what's been happening in her life that day and pray with her. This will build a special bond with her as she understands that you not only care for her and pray with her when you're at home, but when you're gone as well.

- Encourage your child to draw a picture of her prayer with a one-sentence verse or prayer written below it.

- Pray for and with your child long before she's old enough to understand. While bathing your baby, thank God for her perfect body and developing mind. When your child is sick, pray out loud with her for Jesus to help her feel better. Babies and very young children are learning much more than we can imagine and begin to pick up on special words and a tone of voice associated with talking with our Heavenly Father.

- Before your child can pray himself, keep your prayers on his level. For instance, praying about a two-year-old's potty training is right where he's living and very relevant, even though he may not be able to verbalize it himself.

- Running late getting your child to soccer practice or music lessons? Pray together as you're driving. It'll soothe both your nerves and can address the concerns that may be associated with wherever you're going.

- Pray through the newspaper. Read stories that are of interest to your child and then pray for the people involved in that incident.

- Pray through your photo album. As you look through it and recall incidents that happened with friends and family, take a few minutes to pray for the people involved.

- Pray for the needs of someone and then help your child write a note or draw a picture to send to that person. If Grandma has been sick, pray for her and then send her a note letting her know that you've been praying for her.

- Encourage your child to write a prayer poem.

- Call attention to the beauty in nature that God created and thank Him for it. When the leaves are at their peak color in the fall, plan a family picnic. Walk through the falling leaves, compare their shapes and colors and talk about the fact that God made them all different and unique. Thank Him for our world and the beauty around us. Or when you see a beautiful rainbow discuss the fact that it's God's promise never to flood the entire earth again. What an example of His faithfulness to His promises!

- Celebrate the special happy times in your family with prayer – a new baby, the new school year, a new home, birthdays, weddings or graduations.

- Pray with your child about daily problems or successes as they happen. This will help make prayer a natural part of her day.

- When leaving for school, remind your child that he can pray silently during the day regarding his needs – tests, a difficult classmate, fears, etc.

- Pray with your child at spontaneous moments. When admiring a beautiful flower or a new puppy, take a moment to talk about the fact that God made these special things and thank Him for them.

- Bedtime is a good time to pray, but not the best time if your child is very sleepy or tired. Instead, try starting the day with prayer.

- Pray for your neighbors. Start by making sure you have met them with your child and you know a little about them. You could take a picture of their house and post it on a bulletin board along with their names underneath. You might especially pray for those neighbors who have children about the same age as your kids. As you get to know them, you might even want to tell them you are praying for them and invite them to share their concerns with you.

- Always pray before meals. Teach your child to thank God for her food when she is very small and ask her to take her turn in praying before family meals.

- Assure your older child that God understands and is concerned about his special needs – feelings he doesn't always understand, friendship, the opposite sex, etc. Encourage him to pray about these concerns. When he confides in you about concerns such as these, take them seriously. Discuss them, pray with him, and assure him that you'll be praying for him.

- Make prayer an important part of your Thanksgiving celebrations. Involve your whole family – even guests – as you center your thoughts on thanking God for His faithfulness and for things you may have taken for granted. Give each person a small piece of paper and ask them to write down the two things they are most thankful for. Put the papers in a small bowl, shake them up and ask each person to draw one out. Then invite each individual to pray a one or two sentence prayer, thanking God for what they've read on their paper.

- Buy *My Prayer Journal – A Keepsake for Kids Who Love the Lord* (Legacy Press) for your child to record prayer requests and answers.

- As adults, our work occupies the majority of our waking hours. The same is true of school for children. All of the work and learning that takes place, both academically and in their relationships with friends and teachers, is top-priority to the child. This is their world! We would pray with our kids just before they went out the door to school – a prayer about the things that concerned them for that day. There was security and strength in knowing God was aware of their needs and would help them during the day.

- Throw an answer party when God has specifically answered a major prayer concern. When Dad has gotten the new job, grandma's come home from the hospital, a military family member returns from overseas safely or sister is accepted at her first-choice college, celebrate the way God has worked through your prayers. Invite all the people involved in the answer to your house, plan a special meal and praise the Lord together. Hold hands and pray around the circle, thanking God for his faithfulness and answer.

Helping Your Child Grow Spiritually Through
CHURCH

While the primary responsibility for the spiritual growth of your child rests with you as parents, your church is a great place to have your teachings reinforced on a regular basis. You and your church should be working hand-in-hand to provide avenues through which your child can develop spiritually. Depending on how many programs and activities are available for your child's age, it may not be advisable to be involved in all of them. But determine which ones are important to help you reach the SMS you've written and then provide those to your child.

- Be sure your child attends Sunday school and church with you regularly. He needs to feel that this is a warm, loving and important part of life.

- Pray for your minister and his family. If there are special needs mentioned, add them to your prayer list and be consistent in praying for them with your child.

- Encourage your child to listen for at least one point from each message that you can discuss together at home. Dan learned this valuable lesson while attending college. He was serving on the chapel committee and felt it was his "duty" to share with the professor and other committee members that the chapel services were dry and boring and something had to be done. Very wisely, that professor challenged him to listen with the purpose of coming away with just one specific point from each message. It completely changed his attitude and is a technique that we have found applies today as well.

- Let your child dress appropriately casual for church. This should not be a "dress to stress" situation.

- Always let your child hear you speak highly of your pastor and church staff. Never criticize them or say something to lead your child to believe they are doing a poor job.

- Is someone sick or are there circumstances that don't permit you to attend church? Have your own family church service. Ask each child to participate by leading some aspect of your worship time. This could also be a special worship time when you're on vacation.

- Encourage friendships that your child makes with others from your church. Use this as a springboard to learn to know the other family. Kids who have strong friendships with others from church find them to be a great support during their week at school. Having good friends from church will also encourage your child (especially older children and teenagers) to get involved in activities the church offers for their age group.

- If your church provides a children's church service, encourage your child to attend it rather than sitting with you in the adult service. These activities are directed to the age of the children involved and will contribute to learning that church is enjoyable and fulfilling.

- Talk about the upcoming service on your way to church. Let your child see that you are anticipating this time of worship with other believers.

- Talk about your child's Sunday school or children's church activities. Read the take-home stories or materials out loud together.

- Encourage your child to volunteer with you in church-sponsored programs. For instance, if your church is providing a hot Thanksgiving meal for the homeless, ask your child to help you in the serving line. If you are making food and gift baskets for poor families in your area for Christmas, involve her in selecting the gifts and then take her along to deliver the baskets.

- Show by your example that being involved in the activities of the church is important. Make sure your child is involved in groups that are appropriate for his age level, such as:

  Sunday school
  Children's church
  Children's choir
  Vacation Bible school
  Camp
  Youth programs, meetings and parties
  Club programs

Barbie especially enjoyed going to Pioneer Girls and Scott attended Boys Brigade. He would come home quite excited about the things they were doing. It was his first time to experience the fact that spiritual teaching and learning is not the only thing that can happen in church. He would proudly show us the things they were doing and making. In fact, we still have a little shelf that he made while attending that club program.

Helping Your Child Grow Spiritually Through

FAMILY DEVOTIONS

. . . .  . . . .

In the hectic, busy schedule of most families, maintaining a daily family devotional time is very difficult. Not only is time an issue, but the effort and determination to keep it regular and interesting is a challenge. I believe there are two things that can help make it a realistic goal. First, if you feel that you have a lack of time and/or commitment to having daily family devotions, admit it. Ask God to give you the desire and the time to do it. Second, make a determined commitment that this important area of your family life will take a priority. It may mean changing schedules of some family members but it will be well worth it. Sharing together like this will not only contribute to your child's spiritual growth but will spill over into other areas as you are bonded together as a family. Communicating together on a spiritual level will generate trust that will help build communication in other areas.

- Establish a devotional time when all members of the family can be present, such as following the evening meal. Plan this time carefully to make it meaningful and interesting for everyone.

- Try planning your family devotions around a theme for a whole month, such as love – God's love for us, our love for Him, our love for others, and love for our families. Choose scripture readings accordingly and brainstorm with your family ways that you can show love to God, others and family members.

- Ask your child to take an active part in your family devotional times. As he is able, let him read scripture or a Bible story, lead in a hymn or chorus, or lead in prayer. He will enjoy it much more and will learn more by actively participating rather than being a spectator.

- Plan the length of your devotional time with the attention span of your child as a guide. It's not realistic to expect a four-year-old to sit quietly for a half hour or more.

- Use devotional books which are child centered in their emphasis such as:
    The One Year Book of Family Devotions, Vol. 1-3 (Tyndale)
    Little Visits Every Day – Ages 4-7 (Concordia)
    Little Visits With God (Concordia)
    Little Visits With Jesus (Concordia)
    Little Visits for Toddlers – Ages 0-3 (Concordia)
    Little Visits for Families – Ages 7-10 (Concordia)
    Sticky Situations (Tyndale)
    The One Year Book of Devotions for Kids, Vol. 1-3 (Tyndale)
    Family Walk – Ages 10+ (Walk Thru the Bible)
    I Want to Know Series – Ages 7-10 (Zondervan)

- Ask your pastor for information on monthly or quarterly devotional guides produced by your denominational headquarters. A non-denominational quarterly devotional magazine that we enjoyed is *Our Daily Bread* (Discovery House).

- Try using a responsive reading occasionally. Select a portion of scripture and ask one person to read one verse and everyone else read the next in unison. Or use a scripture such as Psalms 136 with one person reading the new thought and everyone reading the response - *His love endures forever* – in unison.

- Plan your devotional time for a month in advance. Keep this time fresh and different. One month you could have it on the patio after the evening meal; another month have it at the park; or in December have it in the family room around the Christmas tree.

- Another way to build devotions around a theme is to capitalize on upcoming holidays. For instance, during the weeks preceding Easter you could select materials that all relate to Christ's death, burial and resurrection. During the weeks before Christmas you could purchase an Advent wreath and use scripture readings appropriate to the symbolism of each candle. November could be devoted to special scriptures and activities promoting a thankful spirit.

- Have a family communion service. This is particularly effective when your church is observing communion the following Sunday and is a good time to teach your child what it means and who can participate. Children can be confused about this important aspect of worship, but the service is not the time or place to answer their questions. Having your own service at home where he'll feel free to voice his questions and concerns will help make communion a very meaningful part of corporate worship.

- As an alternative to family devotions, create a special family night using the ideas in the *Family Night Tool Chest Series* (Chariot Victor).

- Use variety in your family worship: review memory verses or use audio tapes, arts and craft projects, puppets, stories, etc. Keep it informal and child-centered.

Helping Your Child Grow Spiritually Through
BOOKS AND MAGAZINES

The number of Christian books for children has exploded in the last few years. More and more publishers are convinced of the value of providing quality materials and children are reaping the benefits. Books that are carefully chosen for your child's age will be read over and over again.

Reading has always had a high priority in our family. When the kids were very young we began reading to them. We would check books out of the library but would also buy books that would contribute to their spiritual and character development. We started by reading them Bible stories with lots of pictures before they went to bed at night. For Christmas at least one book would be included in their stockings. We would also use a new book as a reward for other things, such as consistent piano practicing over a specified length of time. *The Chronicles of Narnia* (HarperCollins Publisher) were some of their favorites and even now, as adults, they will occasionally reread one of those classics. We also tried to find Christian magazines for their age. They enjoyed receiving the magazines and it made them even more special because they came in the mail with their name on it. There really is no substitute for flooding your child's mind and heart with good things to read and the earlier you start, the better!

- The variety of good Christian literature available includes fiction, adventure, biographies, picture books, mysteries, novels, devotionals, Bible study, books to help them face fears or problems, animal stories, autobiographies, character building stories and books that answer questions that concern them. Try to give your child a good variety!

- If your church has a library, make a habit of checking out books with your child. This is a wonderful source of quality materials and does not involve any expense to you.

- Ask someone on your church staff for magazines that your denominational headquarters produces or ones that your church recommends. A couple that are available from Focus on the Family are:
    Clubhouse Jr. – Ages 4-8
    Clubhouse – Ages 8-12

- Buy and read to your child from a Bible story book like:
    The Beginners Bible – Ages 3-8 (Multnomah)
    The Children's Bible Story Book – Ages 3-8
        (Thomas Nelson)
    The Bible in Pictures for Little Eyes (Moody)
    Read With Me Bible – Ages 4-8 (Zondervan)
    The Children's Bible in 365 Stories (Lion Publishing)
    Hurlburt's Story of the Bible (Zondervan)
    Little Girls Bible Storybook for Mothers & Daughters –
        Ages 4-7 (Baker)
    God's Story – Ages 5-8 (Tyndale)
    The Amazing Treasure Bible (Zondervan)
    The Rhyme Bible Story Book (Multnomah)
    The Beginners Bible – Ages 2-6 (Zondervan)
    The Children's Discovery Bible – Ages 3-6 (Chariot Victor)
    The Praise Bible – Ages 2-6 (WaterBrook)
    My First Bible in Pictures – Ages Birth-3 (Tyndale)

- Introduce books to your child specifically for the purpose of building character. Some suggested titles are:
    Uncle Arthur's Bedtime Stories Classics, Vol. 1-5
        (Review & Herald Publishing)
    A Child's First Steps to Virtue (Harvest House)
    The Children's Book of Virtues (Simon & Schuster)

- Help your child become more excited about the Bible by buying him *The Picture Bible* or *The New Testament Picture Bible* (David C. Cook). These books tell the Bible stories in comic strip format and are in full color.

- Encourage your child to read biographies of great Christians, such as the series published by Barbour Publishing: *Billy Sunday, Billy Graham, Corrie Ten Boom, David Brainerd, Hudson Taylor, Jim Elliot* and *Luis Palau.*

- Read a book together during the Christmas season. Select one that has several chapters that you can complete by reading one chapter each evening.

- Help your child answer some of her questions with books like:
    The Wonder Book – Answers to Kids Questions
        (Child Evangelism)
    The Big Book of Questions and Answers
        (Christian Focus Publications)
    What is God Like? (Tyndale)

Helping Your Child Grow Spiritually Through
AUDIO TAPES

The proliferation of children's videos has made it harder to find character building or Bible story audio tapes. However, it's worth the effort to find them when available because there are some benefits to audio over video. As a child listens to the story, his mind is creatively visualizing the actions about which he is hearing. This kind of material stimulates his thinking skills as he seeks to create a mental picture of what's happening in the story.

• Dan has loved the state fair ever since I've know him. He enjoys roaming from one building to the next to see what every booth has to offer. On a cool, rainy September evening, we decided to get a baby-sitter for the kids and treat ourselves to a night out at the Minnesota state fair. Our intentions were very clear – we were just looking, not buying anything. Of course that wasn't too hard to figure out, since we left home with just enough cash to park and get tickets into the fair. We didn't even have enough extra for a corny dog or cotton candy.

We had a great time going from place to place, huddling together under our umbrella as we ran to the next building. We browsed through everything from the animal barns and farm equipment to the vendors offering imported fineries. Then we came to a booth that really caught our attention. As we started to browse, the gentleman in the booth began to tell us about his product. The more he told us, the more interested we became. Before the evening was over, we had purchased a *Bible in Drama Library* (Christian Educational Services) – all 52 audio tapes – on time with no interest! These Bible stories are beautifully recorded by professional actors and actresses and are complete with sound effects and music. Later we also purchased their 64-tape *Character Building Library*. These two libraries of audio tapes were some of the most important purchases we ever made for our kids and became very instrumental in their spiritual development!

We bought each of them a small cassette player and every night they could choose whatever story they'd like to listen to before going to sleep. (The bonus was that it also gave them time to relax and settle down from their play or homework and be ready to go to sleep.) We also listened to them as a family in the car going down the road on trips. In fact, the kids even listened to them while they made the 900-mile trips back to college. Also, since many of the tapes in the Character Building series are stories of real people in history, they would use them when doing a special report in school. I urge you to consider these cassettes for your children. They are the best I have heard!

- Other cassette tapes and CDs that are available are:
    24 Dramatized Bible Stories on 12 Cassettes
        (Christian Duplications)
    Fill Up On God's Word – Bible Truths for Children in 12
        Tapes (Christian Duplications)
    The Easter Lily – Tape and Book (Brentwood–Benson)
    Bible Stories for the Family Series (Simitar Entertainment)
    Mark Lowry's Cassette and Book Series
        (Gaither Collections)
    Adventures in Odyssey Series (Focus on the Family)

- The two cassettes that come in the package with the book by Charles Swindoll, *Paw Paw Chuck's Big Ideas in the Bible,* for 4 to 9-year-olds, are another great tape resource. (Word)

. . . .
Helping Your Child Grow Spiritually Through
VIDEO TAPES
. . . .

As visual communications continue to explode in almost every area of the marketplace, Christian video companies are seeking to keep pace with other industries. More children's videos with good positive messages are being produced each year. These can be a great form of learning and entertainment with values that your family can embrace. They can also be a positive influence on your child's friends when they are in your home.

• Some videos to consider buying for your child are:

Character building and reinforcing Christian values:
   McGee and Me Series – Ages 5-15 (Focus on the Family)
   Adventures in Odyssey Series – Ages 8+
      (Focus on the Family)
   Quigley's Village Series (Zondervan)
   The Donut Man Series – Ages 2-8 (Integrity Music)
   The Chronicles of Narnia Series (Multnomah)
   Veggie Tales Series (Word)
   The Simple Grand Quigley Band Series – Ages 2-7
      (Zondervan)
   Bibleman Series Ages 3-9 (Pamplin)
   Kingdom Adventure Series (Tyndale)
   Fabulicious Day Series – Age 2-6 (Chariot Victor)
   Guidepost's Junction – *True Stories to Help Build Character*
      (Sparrow)
   Adventures from the Book of Virtues
      (Porch Light Entertainment)

Science and the Bible:
  Newton's Workshop Series – Ages 4+ (Moody)

Prayer:
  Time to Pray: The Adventures of Prayer Bear, Vol. 1-3
    (Sparrow)

Bible Stories:
  The Beginners Bible Series (Word)
  The Storykeepers Series – Ages 6-12 (Zondervan)
  Superbook Video Bible Series (Tyndale)

Music:
  Kids Sing Praise Series (Brentwood-Benson)
  Hide 'Em In Your Heart Series (Sparrow) *
  Cedarmont Kids Series (Brentwood-Benson)
  Psalty's Series (Word)
  Gaither Kids Series (Gaither Collection)
  25 Bible Action Songs Kids Love to Sing (Straightway)
  My First Hymnal (Henley Productions)

• Sometimes videos are available to rent through Christian
  bookstores or they may be a part of your church library.
  A few of the regular rental stores may carry some Bible
  story or character building drama videos as well.

* Abby, our three-year-old granddaughter loves these!!

Helping Your Child Grow Spiritually Through
MISSIONS AND OUTREACH

In years gone by, the term "missions" had an immediate connotation of missionaries going to foreign countries to tell people of Christ. While it still has the same meaning, it is also a much larger term to include mission and outreach opportunities close to home. Reaching out to others can include a wide variety of ways from volunteering at a food pantry to going on a short term mission trip; from visiting shut-ins to helping in relief efforts overseas. The one constant feature of all missions and outreach efforts is the attitude and desire to help others know of Christ through love and involvement.

- To help your child develop a "spirit of ministry" to others, visit the elderly in an assisted living or nursing home. We began doing this with our kids when they were only about 3, 5 and 7 years old. We would talk to the residents and then have a little program for them. The kids would sing a few songs and choruses, we'd sing as a family and then Dan would give a short devotional. The elderly were delighted to have children around and wanted to hug and talk to them. We helped bring a bit of cheer to these people, many of whom rarely had children visit them, and it was a great learning and stretching experience for our family as well.

- Your response to someone who is of another race, handicapped, sick or in the hospital will teach your child volumes. Children are curious about others who appear to be different but are accepting if they sense that kind of attitude in their parents.

- Support an overseas missionary family financially, with your prayers and by writing to them faithfully. Make a scrapbook or bulletin board display with pictures of their family and their work. If you don't know a missionary family, ask one of your church staff members for suggested names from your church or denominational missionary program.

- Put a map of the world on your wall or bulletin board with missionary families' pictures posted on it.

- Study a specific mission field with your child. Make a salt map (a mixture of salt and water to make a stiff consistency) of the area being studied and research the people, culture, missionaries and mission projects.

- Help your child collect used eyeglasses to give to the *Christian Medical and Dental Society*. This organization gives the glasses to people in other countries where their mission trips are conducted. This project could expand to include your child's Sunday school department, club program or even the entire church.

- Encourage your child to join with you in befriending a mentally handicapped person who needs help. If you don't know anyone, there is an organization called *Best Buddies* that matches volunteers with handicapped persons.

- Help your child organize a canned food drive to restock the food pantry at your church or a food pantry in your area. It could include just your neighborhood or could be expanded to your child's Sunday school class, friends, club members or even the entire church. Work with your child in loading the food and delivering it to the designated food pantry.

- Obtain the names of home-bound individuals from your church staff and volunteer to deliver them a hot meal once a week. Involve your child in preparing and delivering the meal. Stay a few minutes at the time of the delivery to encourage the home-bound person and build a friendship.

- During the summer, find a nursing home where your child can volunteer weekly. Help her think of ways she can encourage the residents – bring each a fresh flower or a warm homemade cookie, read to them, write notes to one of their family members for them, bring each a picture that she's drawn, etc.

- If your child's grandparents live a long distance from you, he could adopt a grandparent. Both generations benefit from the interaction with one another. He could help the new grandparent with their grocery shopping; they could work together on a craft or make cookies together; the new grandparent might join your family in going out to eat occasionally, etc. In short, incorporate the older person into your family and encourage your child to be used to bring joy to that person as well.

- Let each family member make a quilt block of their choosing using crayons that can be set with a hot iron. Quilt them together into a baby quilt and donate it to your crisis pregnancy center.

- Encourage your child to join you in working with a refugee family to help them become accustomed to life in the United States. You can find a family in your area who needs help by contacting *World Relief Corporation, Immigration and Refugee Services of America, International Rescue Committee,* or *Church World Service.*

- Let your child volunteer to check out and deliver library books to home-bound people in your church or neighborhood.

- Take your child to visit the children's floor of your local hospital. Plan ahead to bring something small for each patient, such as a picture your child has colored, a small toy or craft item you've made together or a balloon.

- As our kids grew older, we gave them a substantial allowance and they were responsible for all their own clothes, school supplies and lunches, entertainment, etc. Scott decided that he'd like to use some of his money to adopt an orphan from another country. He sent in the card and received his packet with information about a little boy about eight years old living in Mexico. Each month he sent in his support money and lovingly talked about the child as "my kid." It was a great experience that made him feel responsible and that his money was being used in a tangible, specific way to help this little fellow. You could encourage your older child to do the same thing, or perhaps you'd like to adopt one or more of these needy children as a family. Three ministries that work with children overseas are *World Vision, Compassion,* and *Food for the Hungry.*

Helping Your Child Grow Spiritually Through
MUSIC

Everyone enjoys music and there are many different kinds and styles of both secular and religious music from which to choose. Listening to music should be a pleasurable experience, with the lyrics producing a positive influence in the person's life. Whether it's soft music to help quiet a crying baby or the loud sounds of a contemporary Christian artist on the CD player in your child's room, the music sends a strong message to the listener's mind and heart.

• Surround your child with good Christian music through cassette tapes, CDs, videos and your Christian radio station. The more he hears quality music with a positive message the more it will become engrained in his mind. Begin early to encourage him to listen to the words of the songs. Laying a foundation of good music when your child is young will help guide him in the choices he makes as a teenager.

• Learn a new song that your child is singing in church, children's choir or Sunday school.

• Visualize a new hymn or chorus using pictures from magazines to show the actions mentioned in the words.

• Play cassettes or CDs of children's songs while your toddler is playing, while riding in the car together, and when you put her down for a nap or for the night.

- Instead of saying grace before a meal, sing a chorus, the verse of a hymn or the Doxology occasionally.

- We really tried to encourage our kids to listen to the lyrics of a song first and ask themselves questions like "Are the words wholesome?" and "Will listening to them make a positive impression on my mind?" We talked not only about secular music but also about contemporary Christian music. Rather than condemning certain music, we tried to listen with them and make intelligent choices. Those conversations strengthened our communication and we were amazed at what wise choices they came to make. Even the contemporary religious songs had to pass Judy's scrutiny and there were several times when she'd make a comment like, "That's nice music but it's sure bad theology!" I experienced an added benefit personally as I began to listen to new styles and found my taste in music broadened.

- When our children were quite young we were invited to dinner at the home of some new friends. They introduced us to a table blessing that we could sing together. In fact, even now when we're all together we sometimes sing this blessing. The words are sung to the tune of *Edelweiss* from *The Sound of Music.*

> Bless our friends, bless our food.
>> Come O Lord and sit with us.
> May our talk glow with peace
>> May Your love surround us.
> Friendship and love, may it bloom and grow
>> Bloom and grow forever.
> Bless our friends, bless our food.
>> Come O Lord and sit with us!

- There are many wonderful children's audio tapes and CDs available. Consider buying some of these for your child:

Hide 'Em In Your Heart, Vol. 1-3 (Sparrow)
Cedarmont Kids Series (Brentwood-Benson)
Psalty's Series (Word)
My First Hymnal (Henley Productions)
Kids Sing Praise Series (Brentwood-Benson)
America's 25 Favorite Praise & Worship Choruses for Kids
    (Brentwood-Benson)
Angels All Around Series (Word)
Songfest, Vol. 1-2 (Chariot Victor)
Great Songs for Kids Series (Word)
The Beginners Bible Songs for Young Children
    (Rhino Records)
Heaven's Sake Kids (Sparrow)
Cedarmont Kids Series (Brentwood-Benson)
Kid's Collection Series (Brentwood-Benson)
Kids on the Rock (Gospel Light)
Veggie Tales Series – With book – Ages 3+ (Word)
Sunday School Favorites Series (Word)

Helping Your Child Grow Spiritually Through
SPECIAL EVENTS

Any event is worth attending that will help teach your child the values and spiritual lessons you have determined are important to you. Three or four of these events each year could make an indelible impression on him. Many important decisions such as a specific commitment, choice of a college, or career choice can be traced to the impact a special event made on a person. (While in 7th grade, I attended a college choir concert in our community and decided that is where I wanted to go to college!) An added benefit to the spiritual value is the exposure you will give him to a variety of different people and opportunities.

• With your child, go to see or attend events such as:
    A concert featuring a Christian artist
    A Christian film or video showing
    A Holy Land exhibit
    An event featuring a pro athlete giving his/her testimony
    A concert by a college choir or ensemble
    A banquet
    A combined service of churches in the community at Easter, Thanksgiving or Christmas
    The grand opening of a Christian bookstore
    An Easter sunrise service
    A dedication service for a church building or property
    An ordination service
    A live drama presentation
    A display at a museum which depicts Christian art and sculpture

Helping Your Child Grow Spiritually Through

ACTIVITIES

. . . . ❧ . . . .

Many things in life can be learned better and in a much more enjoyable way by making a special activity out of it. Teachers in school recognize this fact very clearly when they schedule unique learning projects or field trips. When Judy was in second grade she was studying farms. Her teacher could have just talked about farms and to most of these city kids it probably wouldn't have made much sense. Instead, the assignment was for each student to make their own farm. Judy started by finding a box with about three-inch sides, filling it with dirt. I was raised on a wheat and cattle ranch in northeastern Montana, so on our visits to Grandpa and Grandma, Judy had learned quite a bit about the farm. She carefully mapped out where the farm buildings should be situated and then where the fields would be planted in her box. She called Grandpa Brown and asked him to send her some wheat, corn and oat seeds to plant in her fields. She'll never forget that project and the fun she had doing it. More importantly, she learned much more than she would have just reading her textbook or hearing her teacher talk about it. Hands-on activities are effective learning tools!

- Make a scrapbook of Sunday school papers, church bulletins, vacation Bible school papers, or materials from a missionary conference.

- Plan a special party when your child can invite his friends. Use ideas from a book such as:
    Parties With a Purpose Ages 2-15 (Thomas Nelson)
    Party! Party! (Group)

- Teach your child to do things for others to show her thoughtfulness. Let her start by baking a cake for your birthday.

- Plan a project on Bible characters. For example, a note-book with a character a week could be made. Your child could draw pictures for it, cut out pictures or write short stories about each character. It could also be integrated into your family devotional times.

- Decorate your child's room with posters, pictures or paint-ings depicting biblical truths.

- Make a study and scrapbook of different trees and herbs of Israel.

- Help your child make a relief map of Israel (Palestine) using a mixture of salt, water, flour, bits of newspaper, food coloring, paste and essence of cloves.

- Adopt a needy family for Thanksgiving or Christmas, preferably one with a child about the age of your child. Shop for gifts for the adopted family and choose grocer-ies that you can buy for their holiday dinner. Deliver your gifts of cheer as a family.

- Lead your child to a feeling of awe and wonder when looking at nature, such as the intricate design of a newly opened flower, a beautiful sunset or a colorful rainbow.

- Buy and encourage Bible related or character building activities such as crossword puzzles, word-find books, quiz books, coloring books, dot-to-dot books, riddle books, hidden picture books, stickers and sticker books, Bible story figures, peel and play activity sets, stencils, paint with water books or invisible ink game books.

- Check the children's ministry section of your local Christian bookstore for materials that you can use at home as well, such as:
  > *Bible Time Crafts Your Kids Will Love* – Ages 6-12
  >> (Group)
  > *Forget-Me-Not Bible Story Activities* (Group)
  > *More Than Mud Pies – Bible Learning Crafts & Games for Preschoolers* (Group)
  > *The Big Book of Bible Games* – Ages 6-12
  >> (Gospel Light)
  > *Nature Crafts for Children* – Ages 3+ (Baker)
  > *Value Builders Series* – Ages 6-12 (David C. Cook)
  > *Crafts and More* (Group)

- Buy your child Christian testimony items such as a cross necklace or earrings, WWJD jewelry, bookmark or key chain, or a Veggie Tales T-shirt.

- There are many games and learning activities available on CD-ROM. Consider purchasing some such as:
  > *Bible Baseball* (Baker)
  > *Bible Coloring Book* (Baker)
  > *Bible Activities on CD-ROM* (Baker)
  > *My First Bible Games* – Ages 4-8 (Chariot Victor)
  > *Games, Puzzles and More* (Baker)
  > *Ultimate Bible Games Series* (Logos Productions)
  > *Bible Time Fun* – Ages 4-12
  >> (Bridgestone Multimedia Group)
  > *Family Bible Game Collection on 5 CD-ROMs* – Ages 7+
  >> (Good News Software)

- Plan a traditional Easter egg hunt for your child and include in the basket a copy of the Gospel of John. After all the eggs have been found, read the story of the resurrection together in John 20.

- Play a game together as a family such as:
  Kids Bible Challenge – Ages 6-12 (Chariot Victor)
  Life Stories . . . Remember the Time – Ages 8-Adult
    (Standard)
  Kids Choices – Ages 6-12 (Chariot Victor)
  Noah's Memory Match-Up Game – Ages 3+
    (Chariot Victor)
  WWJD – What Would Jesus Do? – The Game (Cadaco)
  The Game of Scattergories – Bible Edition – Ages 8+
    (Cactus)
  *Redemption – A Collectible Trading Card Game Based on
    the Bible* (Cactus)
  Bible Treasure Hunt – Ages 10+ (Standard)
  Bible Baseball (Standard)
  Jacob's Ladder – Ages 8-12 (Standard)
  Bibleopoly – Ages 8+ (Late for the Sky)
  Money Matters for Kids – Ages 5-10 (Chariot Victor)
  Kids Bible Challenge – Ages 6-12 (Chariot Victor)
  Bible Scrabble – Ages 10+
    (Review & Herald Publishing)
  Journey Through Bible Land – Ages 3-6
    (Chariot Victor)
  Glory – Ages 5+ (Grace Publications)
  Noah's Ark Memory Match – Ages 3+
    (Grace Publications)
  Bible Stories Sorting and Matching Game – Ages 4+
    (Grace Publications)
  Bible Categories – Ages 12+ (Chariot Victor)
  Bible Challenge – Ages 10+ (Chariot Victor)
  Bible Charades – Ages 10+ (Chariot Victor)
  Sticky Situations – McGee and Me Game – Ages 6+
    (Tyndale)

- Have a birthday party for Jesus at Christmas time. Let your child help plan and prepare for the party as you discuss appropriate ways to celebrate His birth.

- Celebrate the day your child became a part of God's family by having a spiritual birthday party. Plan a special meal complete with decorations. You might talk about what has happened spiritually during the last year, what your child has learned, how she's matured spiritually and what she'd like to do the next year.

- There are two Christmas traditions that our family especially enjoyed when the children were young. The first one was to make decorations for a nursing home. I would call the activities director of a nursing home to ask if we could make a small decoration to hang on each of the residents' doors. I explained that our young children would be making them and we would like to come and attach them to each door. They were always delighted with my proposal and gladly invited us to come. We would spend two or three evenings together on our family art project. It was always something very simple like cutting out a green Christmas tree or a picture from an old Christmas card, gluing it in the middle of a paper plate, and pulling a piece of yarn through a hole in the top to make a hanger. We had a great time making our projects of love and the next day we went to the nursing home with our decorations and a roll of tape to put them on the doors. In retrospect, I'm sure the elderly people appreciated our homemade efforts, but we were the ones who really benefited. As Christmas neared the next year, one of the first things the kids wanted to do was plan our nursing home decorations.

- Another tradition was to read the Christmas story around the tree – usually every night for at least two or three weeks before Christmas. We would read a different part of it each night – the story of the birth, the announcement to the shepherds or the visit of the wise men. We'd vary it by reading from a Bible story book or a different translation, always trying to make it just a little different. To set the stage, the kids would put on their pajamas and we'd turn off all the lights except those on the tree. Then we'd sit in the glow cast by the flickering lights to read and pray together. In fact, we try to continue this tradition even now in a little different form. Whether it's just our immediate family or we have extended family visiting, Dan and the kids plan a program for Christmas Eve. They get everyone involved in reading, singing or some other creative way to participate. This is a tradition that we still enjoy.

I invite you to try one of these in your family next Christmas or try a new approach that is uniquely yours!

Helping Your Child Grow Spiritually Through
EXAMPLE AND INFLUENCE

How many times have we all heard the saying, "Your actions speak so loud I can't hear what you're saying." This is a very awesome thought when applied to parenting. When our kids were little, having everyone ready to leave for church on time was our goal, but it didn't always happen. I hate to be late anywhere so sometimes I would fuss and fume when things weren't progressing as fast as I thought they should. Then Dan reminded me that being a little late once in a while was not nearly as bad as my frustrated attitude and reactions to the kids. How true!

On numerous occasions we see fathers and sons that are "like two peas in a pod" and marvel at their likenesses. Scott has a way of saying things exactly like Dan; his philosophy of life parallels his Dad's very closely. Sometimes when I've done or said something, Barbie or Judy will say, "That sounds just like Grandma!" And so it goes from one generation to the next and the next. So much of what our children learn is not from the things we say they should or should not do, but from simply absorbing our lifestyle as parents. A high percentage of what they learn is through watching and imitating.

• Let your child see you reading from the Bible with respect and anticipation. He will also learn respect for the Bible by your attitude, how you handle it, how you read it and care for it.

• Recount your own experiences with God. Tell her how you came to accept Christ, answers to prayer, and specific ways in which the Lord has led in your life.

- Hang religious pictures, paintings and plaques in your home.

- Model the importance of Christian stewardship. Let your child see you giving your gifts to God's work. Help her learn what the tithe is and how to figure it from her allowance.

- Teach reverence and respect for church through your own actions.

- Let your child hear and see you pray.

- Talk about spiritual things as naturally as you do about the weather, food or clothes. Cultivate an atmosphere in which communication is common and comfortable. Encourage your child's questions and if you don't know the answer, acknowledge it, but tell him you'll look for the answer with him.

- Be consistent and loving in disciplining your child.

- Show your child how she can have a positive influence on her friends.

- When you have made a mistake be willing to admit it. If it involves your child specifically, be ready to tell him you are sorry.

- Remind your child daily how much you love him and that Jesus loves him also. When tucking him into bed at night give him a big hug and kiss and say, "Jesus loves you and I love you so much. Jesus has made you a very special boy."

Part Three

Getting Started

"If I cannot give my children
a perfect mother I can at least give them
more of the one they've got — and
make that one more loving. I will be available.
I will take time to listen, time to play,
time to be home when they arrive from school,
time to counsel and encourage."

— Ruth Bell Graham

There are times when we all seem to get caught in the trap of good intentions. I intend to start my diet soon – in fact, Monday morning would be a good time. Someday I want to go through all those papers I've saved from each of the kids' 12 years in school and sort them out. Someday! Several years ago I looked through all our photos and put them into albums. I need to update the albums with several hundred more pictures that are lying in my drawer in envelopes – maybe next week! The rocks in the back yard landscaping have weeds growing in them. I intend to pull them sometime before they overtake the rocks. I could go on and on and I'm sure you can identify with me.

Some of the things that seem to get caught in the "good intention" state for an endless amount of time are not really all that important. For instance, if I don't get those school papers sorted for another 10 years, so what? They've been packed safely in boxes for several years already and they'll still be there later. However, if I don't get those weeds pulled soon they're going to be so big that they'll be nearly impossible to handle.

Let's just think for a few minutes about the things that really are important in life. Each individual will have a little different priority list but I think we would agree that the welfare of our children is right at the top. The fact that you are reading this book shows that you are concerned about your child's spiritual development.

Now that you have a SMS for your child (if you haven't finished it, go back to page 17 and do it NOW) and have read some ideas to help you get started, how can they be moved from the list of good intentions to action? Are there some steps to follow to make it easier in our fast-paced schedules?

There are great variances in parents' personalities, habits, priorities and methods of accomplishing their goals. Understanding these differences, I am going to describe three different plans that you could use to get started.

For Those Who Prefer
A DETAILED STRATEGY

Annual Planning Session

Step 1: Begin by buying a spiral notebook and write on the front cover, "Jane's (your child's name) Spiritual Journey." Then write the SMS that you have determined on the first page.

Step 2: Set aside some time specifically for the purpose of mapping out your strategy for planned spiritual growth for the next year. If you're getting this book in the middle of the year begin by planning for the weeks and months left of this year. If possible, get a baby-sitter and go out for the evening – for dinner or coffee, or to a park, lake or other favorite quiet place. Begin by reviewing the SMS that you've written. What have you determined will be your greatest emphasis? How does it fit immediately with the age of your child?

Step 3: Think of all the things you might want to do in each of the 12 areas during the next year. Read back over those suggested in the book and add things of your own as they come to your mind. Make headings in your spiral notebook of each of the areas and list your ideas under each one. Having some ideas in each area helps you approach your child's spiritual growth with a balanced plan. This will help you guard against the tendency to put all the emphasis on one category such as videos or church.

Step 4: Now that you've written down your ideas it's time to get serious about what you're actually going to do. Go back through your lists, study each idea carefully and highlight or put a check mark beside those that you determine you're definitely going to pursue. If you want, write these choices on a separate sheet of your notebook, apart from the lists of ideas.

Step 5: The last step is to decide when you're going to do each thing and write it on a calendar. You may wish to use one by your kitchen table or in your study, but make sure it is very visible and accessible. This calendar will keep you on track and help you accomplish your plans. As in other family activities, you need only check the calendar to see what you need to be doing in this very important area.

If you have decided to memorize a verse a week around the table, now is the time to select the verses. Begin by determining a subject for each month and then choosing four or five verses relating to that subject. Write the reference of the verse for that week on the Sunday square of your calendar. The next Sunday will have the reference for the next verse, etc. We found this to be a very easy way to turn scripture memorization from good intentions to reality. There's a chance you'll forget it if you have to select a new verse every week. But when the decision has been made earlier and the reference is already on the calendar it's much easier to be consistent.

If your child is old enough to join the children's choir at church and you've decided this is something you want to do in the fall, write it into one of the first days of September. If your vacation will take you through Arkansas maybe you'd like to stop in Eureka Springs to see the Passion Play. Write it on your calendar during your vacation time. If you've decided you'd like to buy your child six new videos during the next year, make a notation at the first of every other month.

Try to be realistic in the things you're going to try to do, but at the same time, force yourself to stretch a bit. Don't forget to include on your calendar those intangible reminders to yourself – like continually being aware of your influence, taking time to capture those unplanned moments for great spiritual teaching, or developing your own prayer life.

Be sure to include time in your annual planning session to spend time in prayer for your child. Don't make it so mechanical that you lose the spirit and essence of what you're trying to do.

Monthly Planning Session

Set aside 15-30 minutes on the last day of the month or the first day of the new month to look over your plans. Review your progress from the month before and go over the things that you've written for the next month. Read through the ideas you had listed in your notebook at the beginning of the year and add or subtract anything you feel you might want to change for the next month.

The last step is to keep your calendar in front of you and then JUST DO IT! Take a few minutes at the beginning of each week to review your progress.

For Those Who Prefer
A LITTLE STRUCTURE

Even if you're not the kind of person who enjoys a very detailed strategy for accomplishing your goals, go back and read the previous section if you happened to skip it. This section will give you a plan that may be more your style, but some of the principles that will be used are the same as those already discussed.

Annual Planning Session

Step 1: As in the first plan, begin by buying a spiral notebook, writing "Jane's (your child's name) Spiritual Journey" on the cover and then your SMS on the first page.

Step 2: If at all possible, plan a time away from home when you can concentrate on your plans for the whole next year – or until the end of this year, if you're getting this book somewhere in the middle. Review the SMS you've written for your child. Assess your statement and talk about your child's progress in spiritual growth. Discuss and write in your notebook the general, broad areas that you'd like to see developed during the next year – scripture memory, consistently reading Bible stories and praying before bed, purchasing the *Bible in Drama Library*, or reaching out to the new people moving into your neighborhood. If you have specific things you are sure you want to do, write them down as well.

If you have decided to memorize a verse a week, take time now to at least select the subject areas for each month remaining this year. Then choose the four or five verses that you'll work on this month. If you could select the verses for the next three months now, it would be even better. Our experience is that it's much easier to be consistent if the verses are already there before you.

If you already know that you definitely want to send your child to camp (or any other thing or activity that you're sure of), write it down as a definite and write it on your calendar or put an estimated registration date beside it.

Step 3: Decide specifically what you want to do for this month. Write these items down on your calendar. Remember, writing the things you've decided on the calendar is the first step toward actually putting them into practice. Take a few minutes to pray specifically for your child and the needs she's facing at this point in her life.

Monthly Planning Session

Set aside a few minutes at the end of the month or the first day of the new month to review your progress. Write on your calendar the things you want to do for the next month. If you need help deciding, read back through the ideas in this book or other ideas that you've already jotted down in your notebook.

The last and most important part? JUST DO IT!! Use the predetermined notations on your calendar to keep you on the offense! Determination and perseverance will bring the spiritual growth that you so desire for your child.

. . . .

For Those Who Prefer

A SPONTANEOUS APPROACH

. . . .

If you're the kind of person who finds it difficult to operate under a detailed plan and prefers to just do things as they come, take heart! This plan is for you! There are a few steps you'll need to take, but this is as simple as it gets.

Annual Planning Session

Step 1: Buy your spiral notebook and write on the cover "Jane's (your child's name) Spiritual Journey". Write the SMS that you've already determined on the first page.

Step 2: What a great reason to get a baby-sitter and have a night out! Plan to go someplace you really enjoy but remember your main purpose – to talk about your child's spiritual growth. There are three things you'll want to accomplish. First, read over your child's SMS. Second, promise yourself and each other that you'll make your child's spiritual growth a priority and write down general or specific ideas of things you might want to do. Third, pray that the Lord will keep your promise in the front of your minds and that you'll constantly be aware of opportunities to help your child grow spiritually.

Step 3: Read through the ideas in the 12 areas of this book and/or think of ideas of your own. Jot down the general ideas and then write on your calendar the things you want to do for the following month.

Monthly Planning Session

Set aside a few minutes at the end of the month or the very beginning of the new month to review your progress.

Write on your calendar the things you want to do for the next month.

If you've decided to memorize scripture around the table, select a new subject at the beginning of each month and then choose verses for the month. Or, find a new verse at the beginning of each week or just one a month.

If your church has just announced the formation of a new weekday program, decide if this is something for your child. If so, put the registration date on your calendar. The most important part is to write your plan for the month on your calendar. Then JUST DO IT!

For Everyone Committed To Charting A Spiritual Journey For Their Child

If you don't do all the things you had planned to do, don't get discouraged. Dan and I sometimes chuckle now when we look over our lists from years ago when our children were young. We had incredibly high aspirations and voluminous lists. However, there were some years that we only did about 20% of what we had written down. At first we became very discouraged. Then we realized something. That 20% was more than we would have done if we hadn't thought it through and written our long lists. Also, by going through the process, we were much more aware of unexpected daily occurrences that lent themselves to spiritual lessons.

So keep at it! I'd be the last one to say it's easy. That's just not so. But I can say from experience that those years of planting values and spiritual insights into your children fly by all too quickly. Many times the visible accomplishment and rewards won't come until much later. But when your children reach adulthood and you see them committed to Christ, seeking to live their lives in God's will and involved in the church, it makes every minute invested in their spiritual development more than worth it!

Part Four

Grip Groups To Strengthen
Parenting Skills

"When nothing seems to help, I go
and look at a stonecutter hammering away
at his rock, perhaps a hundred times
without as much as a crack showing in it.
Yet, at the hundred and first blow, it
will split in two, and I know it was not
that blow that did it, but all that
had gone before."

— Jacob A. Riis

GET A GRIP ON PARENTING
IN A GRIP GROUP

More than once I've been ready to hand in my "mother button"! I would have liked to take a break for a few days; to just do what I wanted to do without thought of anyone else, not to have any responsibility or concern for our kids. But once I became a parent it was impossible to change my mind or back out. Because parenting is so long and so permanent, there are going to be occasions when things don't go as well as we'd like them to. Discouragement haunts all of us at times.

One of the best ways to get a grip on being an effective parent is to be part of a GRIP Group –
> **G**rowth
> **R**elationships
> **I**nspiration
> **P**artnership

Growth will come as you seek **R**elationships with other parents, and you'll receive **I**nspiration when you form a **P**artnership with others who are facing similar challenges.

A GRIP Group of Two

A GRIP Group could be as small as two moms or two dads. Having a friend who has a child about the same age as yours is a good sounding board. You can share your ups and downs, your successes and failures, things that are working for you and things that aren't working. Candidly comparing your lives as parents can help each person gain new insights and parenting techniques. The most important part is to find a friend with whom you can pray. Try meeting once a week or just setting aside a specific time to talk together on the phone each week. Commit that you will pray for one another and for each child's needs. Share your joys and concerns about your child and then pray together. The more vulnerable and honest you are able to become with each other, the more encouragement and support you will receive from the relationship.

A GRIP Group of Several

A second way which is very effective is to form a GRIP Group in your church or neighborhood. This is a group of parents (three to ten individuals or three to six couples) who meet together for mutual support, encouragement and prayer. If there is a large number of parents who would like to be part of a group, divide into two groups according to the general ages of the children. Potential GRIP Group members could be found through:

- adult Sunday school classes
- announcements in your church bulletin
- announcements in your church newsletter
- your child's Sunday school class or weekday club
- the church nursery or day care program
- neighborhood Bible study or social gathering

Plan a specific time for the GRIP Group to meet – once a week, every other week, or once a month. You could take turns meeting in participants' homes, at the church in the evening, immediately before or after a regularly scheduled morning or evening service, or right after day care. Find a time that will be the most convenient to the most people.

Each person or couple needs to bring their spiral notebook where they've written their child's SMS and ideas in the 12 areas of growth. The back part of the notebook can be used for ideas they hear during the GRIP Group meeting and also to record the current prayer requests.

Each meeting should generally follow this format:

1. Light refreshments could be served as people arrive.

2. The individual or couple leading the meeting should begin with prayer and possibly scripture or a short devotional. You could have one person or couple who is always the leader, or a different leader could volunteer or be asked to be responsible for the next meeting.

3. The first time the group meets should be used primarily as a get-acquainted time to get to know each parent and their child(ren). Discuss the first section of this book on writing a SMS and ask each person to read the book and complete the SMS for their child before the next meeting if they haven't already done so. At the next meeting ask each person to share what they've written for their child. Go around the group taking turns sharing victories and concerns as well as ideas that are being used effectively. At the meeting at the end of the month, each parent should share some of the things they've planned for the following month. (At first it may be difficult to tell others about difficulties or discouragement, but as one person is willing to be vulnerable, others will begin to feel comfortable enough to share also.) One of the greatest benefits of sharing is the encouragement that comes when you know that others are going through some of the same things. Also, telling others about things that are working well in your family will give them new ideas of things they can try.

4. Update the group on your prayer requests and answers since the last meeting. Be sure to write down new prayer requests as they are mentioned.

5. Allow plenty of time to pray together regarding the needs and requests that have been mentioned. All parents in the group should agree to confidentiality and pledge themselves to help and pray for each other.

Note: A five-session <u>Leader's Guide</u> is provided free from the publisher (see address on last page of book), including discussion questions. Just request a copy and include $3 for postage and handling.

A Final Word –

Physical growth of a child is easy to observe. At certain stages of life it seems that you can almost see them growing as you watch their jeans creep further up toward their knees. Spiritual growth is much more subtle. There could be long periods of time when you wonder if anything is happening. Are any of the values and principles you're trying to teach getting through? Progress may not be visible, but slowly, slowly it's making a difference. Our responsibility is to continue to nurture and feed each child spiritually in order for them to become all God intends them to be.

Rewards are sometimes few and far between in the task of parenting. Our heads tell us that we must keep plodding ahead to help our children become mature, spiritually alive adults. But sometimes our hearts cry out for something visible to show progress being made. Galatians 6:9 promises,

"Let us not become weary in doing good,
for at the proper time we will reap a harvest
if we do not give up."

God has promised that if we continue doing what we know to be right and good, the harvest will come!

As the kids were growing up, Dan tried to teach them the importance of showing their love to me by making or buying me something special for Mother's Day. When they were small he'd take all three of them to the hardware store to find a gift that I would actually use. They reminisce about those shopping excursions with fondness and a fair number of laughs as they recall the little kitchen gadgets they would so carefully select. As they got older the traditional shopping trips with Dad gave way to other ways of expressing love and appreciation.

The first Mother's Day that Barbie was away from home was when she was a freshman in college in Illinois. She found a beautiful, intricately laser cut card and wrote her own sentiments inside. I keep this card in my Bible and will always cherish it!

It says:

> "To one of my best friends in the whole world –
> Thanks for caring for me and loving me.
> Thanks for teaching me about God and His love.
> Thanks for being open-minded
>   without compromising values.
> I love you.
> Love, Barbie"

The rewards do come!

Appendix

Where to Find Products and Services

Throughout this book you have found specific names of organizations and companies. They are listed below in alphabetical order with their addresses and phone numbers. *Note* – while some may not service retail customers, they would be able to recommend a book store or distributor in your area that handles their product or service.

Baker Book House/Revell
PO Box 6287
Grand Rapids, MI 49516
800-877-2665

Barbour Publishing, Inc.
Box 719
Uhrichsville, OH 44683
740-922-6045

Best Buddies International
100 SE Second St., Ste. 1990
Miami, FL 33131
800-89 BUDDY

Betty Lukens
711 Portal St.
Cotati, CA 94931
707-795-2745

Brentwood-Benson Music
365 Great Circle Road
Nashville, TN 37228
800-333-9000

Bridgestone Multimedia Group
300 N. McKemy Ave.
Chandler, AZ 85226
602-940-5777

Brighter Child Interactive
4079 Executive Pkwy., #303
Westerville, OH 43081
614-847-8118

Broadman & Holman Pub.
127 Ninth Ave. N.
Nashville, TN 37234
800-725-5416

Cactus Game Design
1553 S. Military Hwy.
Chesapeake, VA 23320
800-365-1711

Cadaco
4300 W. 47th St.
Chicago, IL 60632
773-927-1500

Chariot Victor Publishing
4050 Lee Vance View
Colorado Springs, CO 80918
800-437-4337

Child Evangelism Fellowship
PO Box 348
Warrenton, MO 63383
314-456-4321

Christian Duplications Int'l
1710 Lee Road
Orlando, FL 32810
407-298-6612

Christian Educational Services
11911 McIntosh Road
Thonotosassa, FL 33592
813-986-4761

Christian Focus Publications
Geanies House
Fearn Tain
Ross-shire IV20 1TW
England
(+44) 1862 871541

Christian Medical & Dental Soc.
Box 5
Bristol, TN 37621
423-844-1000

Church World Service
475 Riverside Dr., Room 664
New York, NY 10115
212-870-3302

Compassion International
PO Box 7000
Colorado Springs, CO 80933
719-594-9900

Concordia Publishing House
3558 S. Jefferson Ave.
St. Louis, MO 63118
800-325-3040

David C. Cook
850 N. Grove Ave.
Elgin, IL 90120
719-536-0100

Discovery House Publishers
PO Box 3566
Grand Rapids, MI 49501
800-653-8333

Focus on the Family Publishing
8605 Explorer Dr.
Colorado Springs, CO 80920
719-531-3496

Food for the Hungry
7729 E. Greenway Rd.
Scottsdale, AZ 85260
602-998-3100

Gaither Collection
Box 178
Alexandria, IN 46001
800-955-8746

Good News Software
1300 Crescent St.
Wheaton, IL 60187
630-682-4300

Gospel Light/Regal Books
2300 Knoll Dr.
Ventura, CA 93003
806-644-9721

Grace Publications
23740 Hawthorne Road
Torrance, CA 90505
310-378-1133

Group Publishing Inc.
1515 Cascade Ave.
Loveland, CO 80538
970-669-3836

HarperCollins Publisher
10 E. 53rd St.
New York, NY 10022
212-207-7000

Harvest House Publishers
1075 Arrowsmith
Eugene, OR 97402
541-343-0123

Heaven Word
2940 Trawick Road, #9
Raleigh, NC 27604
919-876-1124

Henly Productions
Box 40269
Nashville, TN 37204
615-383-8845

Ideal/Instructional Fair
Box 1650
Grand Rapids, MI 49501
800-633-4606

Immigration and Refugee Serv.
1717 Mass. Ave. NW, Ste. 701
Washington, DC 20036
202-797-2105

Integrity Music Co.
1050 5th Ave., #14A
New York, NY 10028
212-348-3990

International Rescue Comm.
122 E. 42nd St., 12th Floor
New York, NY 10168
212-551-3000

Kirkbride Bible Company
Box 606
Indianapolis, IN 46206
800-428-4385

Late for the Sky Production Co.
561 Reading Rd.
Cincinnati, OH 45202
513-721-8124

Legacy Press
PO Box 261129
San Diego, CA 92196
619-578-1273

Lion Publishing plc
Peter's Way
Sandy Lane West
Oxford OX4 5H6
England
(+44) 1865 747550

Little Folk Visuals
39620 Entrepreneur Lane
Palm Desert, CA 92211
760-345-5571

Logos Productions Inc.
6160 Carman Ave. E.
Inver Grove Heights, MN 55076
800-875-6467

Maher Studios
Box 420
Littleton, CO 80160
303-798-6830

Moody Press
820 N. LaSalle Dr.
Chicago, IL 60610
800-678-8812

Multnomah Publishers
PO Box 1720
Sisters, OR 97759
800-929-0910

NavPress Publishing Group
7899 Lexington Dr.
Colorado Springs, CO 80920
800-366-7788

Off the Curb Publishing
306-N West El Norte Pkwy.,
    Ste. 352
Escondido, CA 92026
760-738-7039

One Way Street
PO Box 5077
Englewood, CO 80155
303-790-1188

Pamplin Music Corp.
10209 SE Division St.
Portland, OR 97266
503-251-1555

Parson's Technology
Box 100
Hiawatha, IA 52233
319-395-9626

Porch Light Entertainment
11828 LaGrange Ave.
Los Angeles, CA 90025
310-477-8400

Puppet Factory
117 E. 17th St.
Goodland, KS 67735
785-899-7143

Review & Herald Publishing
55 W. Oak Ridge Dr.
Hagerstown, MD 21740
800-234-7630

Rhino Records
10635 Santa Monica Blvd.
Los Angeles, CA 90025
310-474-4778

Simitar Entertainment, Inc.
5555 Pioneer Creek Dr.
Maple Plain, MN 55359
561-966-8397

Simon & Schuster
1230 Avenue of the Americas
New York, NY 10020
800-223-2336

Son Shine Puppet Co.
PO Box 6203
Rockford, IL 61125
815-965-8080

Sparrow Corporation
PO Box 5010
Brentwood, TN 37024
615-371-6800

Standard Publishing
8121 Hamilton Ave.
Cincinnati, OH 45231
800-542-1301

Straightway, Inc.
Box 74068
Romulus, MI 48174
313-941-4400

Thomas Nelson Publishing
501 Nelson Place
Nashville, TN 37214
800-251-4000

Tyndale House Publishers
PO Box 80
Wheaton, IL 60189
800-323-9400

Walk Thru the Bible
4201 N. Peachtree Rd.
Atlanta, GA 30341
770-458-9300

WaterBrook Press
5446 N. Academy Blvd., # 200
Colorado Springs, CO 80918
719-590-4999

Word Publishing
Box 141000
Nashville, TN 37214
615-902-3400

World Relief Corporation
PO Box WRC
Nyack, NY 10960
914-268-4135

World Vision
Box 9716
Federal Way, WA 98063
253-815-1000

Zondervan Publishing House
5300 Patterson Ave. SE
Grand Rapids, MI 49530
800-727-1309

Only be careful, and watch yourselves
closely so that you do not forget the things your
eyes have seen or let them slip from
our heart as long as you live. Teach them
to your children and to their children
after them. Love the Lord your God with all
your heart and with all your soul and
with all your strength. These commandments
that I give you today are to be upon
your hearts. Impress them on your children.
Talk about them when you sit at home
and when you walk along the road, when you
lie down and when you get up.

Deuteronomy 4:9; 6:5–7

A Piece of Clay

I took a piece of moist clay
And idly fashioned it one day.
And, as my fingers pressed it still,
It moved and yielded to my will.

I came again when days were past,
The bit of clay was hard at last.
The form I gave it, it still bore,
But I could change that form no more.

I took a piece of living clay,
And gently formed it day by day
And molded with my power and art
A young child's soft and yielding heart.

I came again when years were gone,
It was a man I looked upon;
He still that early impress wore,
And I could change him never more.

Author Unknown

CARPENTER SHOP RESOURCES

PO Box 292175
Lewisville, Texas 75029
800-576-6162
www.csre.com